CONSERVATION OF
THE SEA

Text: Rosa Costa-Pau
Illustrations: Estudio Marcel Socías

La Conservación del Mar © Copyright Parramón Ediciones, S. A. Published by Parramón Ediciones, S. A., Barcelona, Spain.

1 3 5 7 9 8 6 4 2

Conservación del mar. English.
  Conservation of the sea.
    p. cm.—(The Junior library of ecology)
  Includes index.
  ISBN 0-7910-2102-5
  1. Marine resources—Juvenile literature. 2. Marine resources conservation—Juvenile literature. [1. Marine pollution. 2. Pollution. 3. Marine resources conservation.] I. Title. II. Series.
  GC1016.5.C6613 1994   93-19872
  333.91'6416—dc20   CIP
                                                  AC

Contents

The Junior Library of Ecology

CONSERVATION OF THE SEA

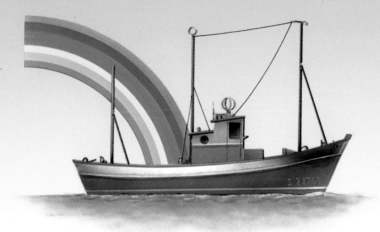

CHELSEA HOUSE PUBLISHERS

New York • Philadelphia

The Sea

Physical Environments

The planet earth has a great variety of physical environments. A physical environment is a place where organisms and creatures live. It may be a field, a forest, a lake, a river, or a sea.

Living beings do not live in isolation from the world that surrounds them. They form part of a whole ecosystem in which they interact with each other and with their physical environment.

Two hundred and fifty million years ago there were no snakes or frogs or even fish on our planet. Over a long period of time measured in millions of years, ancient organisms underwent many changes, which produced the creatures that today inhabit the sea, land, and air.

Life began in the sea. Later on, organisms found their way onto the land and into the air. Each one of these physical environments forms its own natural system with unique characteristics.

▼

From the smallest to the largest. The sea contains a great variety of life-forms, from microscopic plankton to whales.

The Changes in the Sea

Life in the sea today is different from what it must have been when it first began there.

The sea has always been a source of food and energy for human beings, as well as a means of traveling from one place to another. But in modern times the sea has also been used as the world's great rubbish dump. In spite of this, life has managed to continue, thanks to the sea's natural ability to purify itself.

For thousands of years humanity has extracted essential resources from the sea. The peoples of ancient history lived off fish and used the sea as a means of communication and transport. In more recent times, people have begun to extract other kinds of riches, such as oil and various minerals. Today, however, pollution can damage the sea's natural resources.

▼

Industrial waste. Waste that is emptied into rivers is carried out to sea. When a lot of materials are dumped into the sea, the equilibrium between the river and sea can be destroyed.

Sewage. If untreated sewage is emptied into the sea, the microorganisms contained in it can consume the oxygen that fish and marine plant life need to breathe.

Nuclear waste. The dumping of nuclear waste is carried out in some ocean areas. In spite of the precautions taken there have been cases of radiation leakages, putting into question the safety of such dumping.

Means of transport. There is a lot of maritime traffic nowadays, which increases the danger of ocean pollution.

The Sea's Characteristics

● CHLORINE
● SODIUM
● MAGNESIUM
● OTHER SALTS

Salinity

Important components of sea water are salt, gases, and other dissolved substances. Seawater also contains particles of calcium, iron, copper, silver, and even gold.

However, the most abundant element is sodium chloride, or common household salt. The sea's salinity, or salt content, differs from place to place. In polar regions, the sea's salt content is low; on the other hand, salinity is very high in tropical areas. Salinity is related to the water's density. Salty water is denser then water with less salt.

◄ *The degree of salinity of sea water varies in different areas of the oceans. But on average a quart of water contains 1.2 ounces of salt.*

Apart from the different types of salt found in seawater— sodium chloride, magnesium chloride, and other compounds— seawater contains 87% oxygen and 11% hydrogen, by weight. ►

With weak winds, the height of the wave (the distance between the crest and the trough) is shorter than the wave's length (the distance between one crest and another).

If the wind is strong, the wave's height will grow and its length will shorten. The movement of the water then becomes elliptical.

The wind causes the crest of the wave to form foam.

Waves are caused by ► *the wind. The water forms vertical waves, but it is the wind that makes them move. Water particles make waves by moving in circles that progressively take on elliptical shapes when the wind increases its strength or when the wave approaches the shore.*

CREST

TROUGH

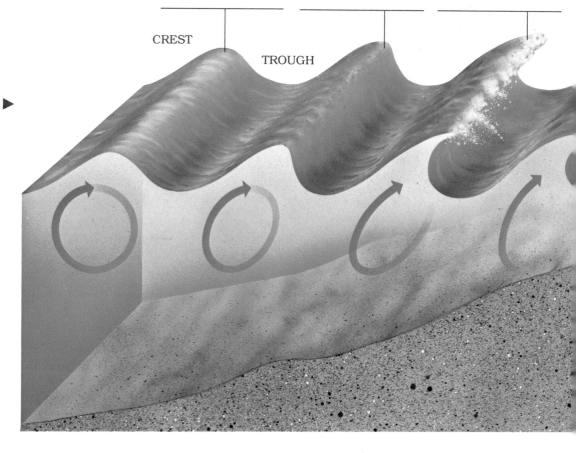

Unlike waves, sea currents create horizontal movements in the water. Some of the main sea currents transport warm waters from the equator to the poles, making the oceans a moderating element of the world's climate.

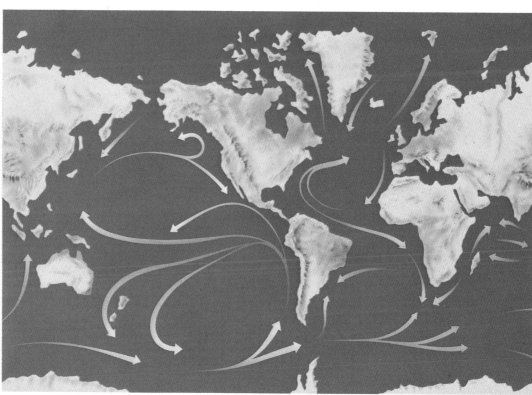

The wave cannot form a complete ellipse on beaches that have a slight slope.

The wave breaks on the beach and the foam breaks up.

Sea Currents

Some sea currents are produced by winds that blow on the sea. But the most important sea currents are produced by differences between the salinity, temperature, and density of the water. Sea currents move the water around, enriching the oceans with oxygen and carbon dioxide.

The oxygen is breathed by fish and other marine life, while carbon dioxide is used in food production and photosynthesis carried out by sea plants.

From the Ocean Depths to the Surface

The Sea's Inhabitants

The deepest parts of the sea are darker and colder.

Some of the creatures that live in the depths are blind. They do not need sight because light never reaches the sea's bottom. These creatures feed on other animals, since plant life can not exist without light.

The sea's surface is home to some very small organisms that contain chlorophyll, just like other green plants. They are known as phytoplankton. Living off phytoplankton are other tiny organisms known as zooplankton.

All sea creatures ultimately depend on phytoplankton for food. The life of these little

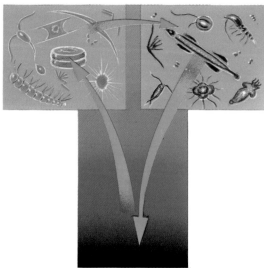

plants depends on the amount of sunlight and the presence of certain mineral elements in the sea. Although sunlight only penetrates the upper parts of the sea and does not go down further than about three hundred feet, minerals are found at the ocean bottom.

The ocean floor can be divided into different regions: the continental shelf, the continental slope, the seabed, and deep ocean trenches.

▼

The continental shelf. This begins at the seashore and descends to 500 to 600 feet below sea level. It is where most fish live and mineral and oil deposits are found.

The continental slope. This region drops swiftly to the ocean floor.

The sea plain. This lies about 9,000 feet below sea level and covers most of the ocean floor.

Ocean islands are the result of volcanic eruptions in the middle of the ocean.

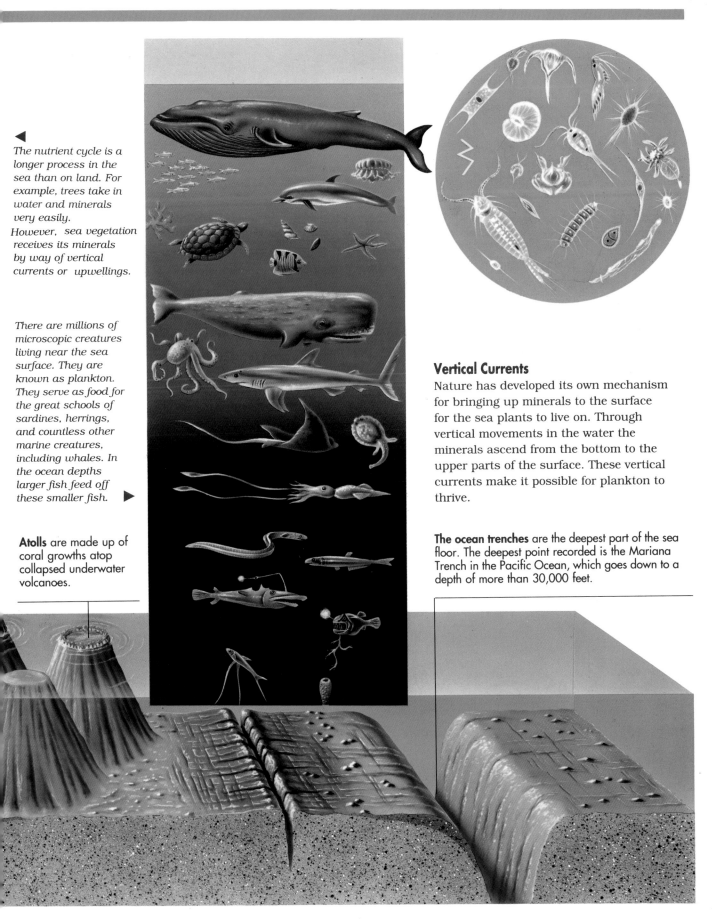

The nutrient cycle is a longer process in the sea than on land. For example, trees take in water and minerals very easily. However, sea vegetation receives its minerals by way of vertical currents or upwellings.

There are millions of microscopic creatures living near the sea surface. They are known as plankton. They serve as food for the great schools of sardines, herrings, and countless other marine creatures, including whales. In the ocean depths larger fish feed off these smaller fish. ▶

Atolls are made up of coral growths atop collapsed underwater volcanoes.

Vertical Currents

Nature has developed its own mechanism for bringing up minerals to the surface for the sea plants to live on. Through vertical movements in the water the minerals ascend from the bottom to the upper parts of the surface. These vertical currents make it possible for plankton to thrive.

The ocean trenches are the deepest part of the sea floor. The deepest point recorded is the Mariana Trench in the Pacific Ocean, which goes down to a depth of more than 30,000 feet.

The Water Cycle

The Seas

It is impossible to find the beginning and end of a sea, because, in reality, all the seas on our planet are one. The waters from one sea are connected to the others.

Water covers three quarters of the earth's surface. People have divided the sea into different oceans and given them names:

the Pacific, the Atlantic, the Indian, the Arctic, and the Antarctic Ocean. Seas and oceans are unique to our planet in the solar system.

About 2.5 billion years ago life began in the sea. Since then, life on earth has been sustained by the existence of the sea.

When snow melts it forms streams and brooks that converge in valleys. They make up minor water systems. Both the overland and underground streams flow to the sea.

Water filters through the different layers of earth, creating underground streams.

The water contained in the clouds can fall in the form of snow or rain.

Water evaporates from damp vegetation on the ground.

The wind blows the clouds toward the continents and the water is released in the form of rain.

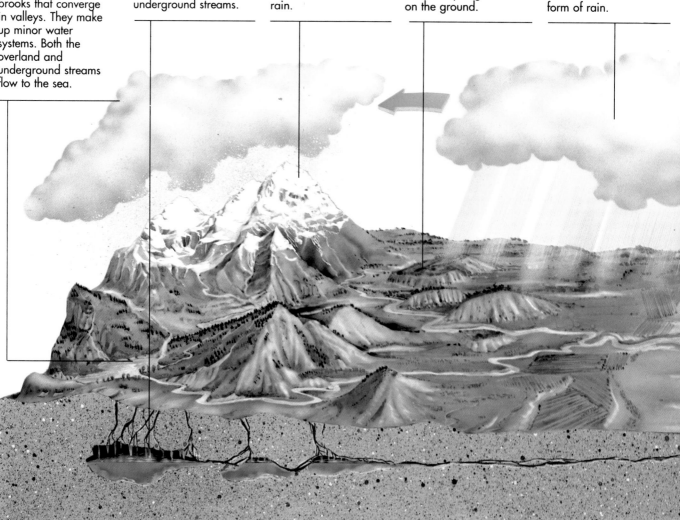

The Water Cycle

Climate, the shape of the mountains, and the way our planet's different creatures live all depend on the sea.

The clouds, the rain, the snow, and the rivers and lakes are created by the action of seawater. The sun heats the seawater, which then evaporates. The water vapor condenses to become clouds, from which rain or snow falls. The water then returns to the sea by way of rivers and streams. Some of the water filters through the ground and forms underground reservoirs. All of this is what is known as the water cycle.

Day after day, year after year, for millions of years, the sun has evaporated seawater and then returned it to the sea along rivers. Water has never stopped renewing itself.

The quantity of the earth's water has remained constant because water is not destroyed when it is used. Water comes to us in the form of clouds, rain, snow, rivers, lakes, and seas.

In this illustration you can see the water cycle. Water undergoes various changes through evaporation of the seas, transpiration of vegetation, condensation of water vapor, and precipitation in the form of rain or snow. Then it completes the cycle by returning to the sea through rivers and streams.

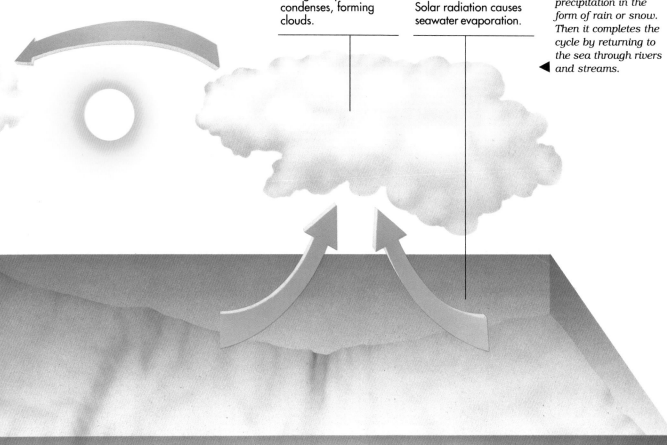

Rising damp air condenses, forming clouds.

Solar radiation causes seawater evaporation.

Water Is Scarce

The Development of Cities

Since ancient times, people have banded together in communities. The smaller communities lived mainly on agriculture and livestock raising. The bigger ones depended on industry and commerce.

Water has been an absolute necessity since the first urban communities were formed. Historically, when a city reached its maximum number of inhabitants, some of those inhabitants would build a new city in an undeveloped area. Uncontrolled urban growth meant serious water supply problems.

Roman cities were built with a sophisticated sewer network. The water supply was ensured with the use of great aqueducts.

▼

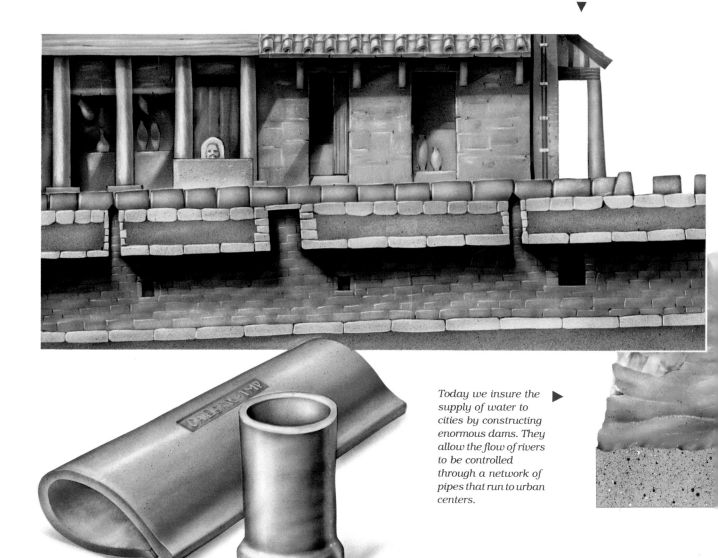

Today we insure the supply of water to cities by constructing enormous dams. They allow the flow of rivers to be controlled through a network of pipes that run to urban centers. ▶

Water Consumption

The enormous cities of Calcutta, Sao Paulo, Hong Kong, and Mexico City have grown more than anyone could have expected. What has happened to their water supply?

Lately, consumption of water worldwide has quadrupled, going from 200 cubic miles to 800 cubic miles. This is not only because of an increasing population but also because today's agricultural systems and industrial processes need more water.

Every day, in every house, people turn on their taps and out flows water from a nearby reservoir. It is the water we consume when we drink, wash, cook, and water the plants.

Canals have been built and rivers diverted; water from underground aquifers has been extracted. But the governments of the countries where water is scarce have to impose restrictions on its use and promote campaigns to cut down on individual water consumption.

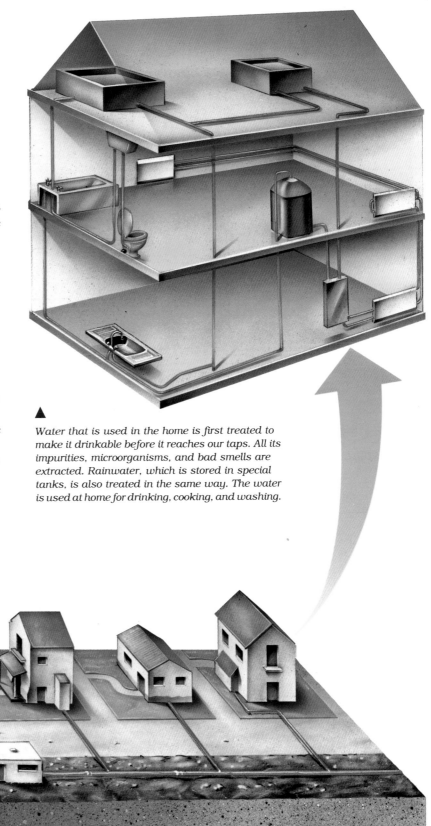

▲
Water that is used in the home is first treated to make it drinkable before it reaches our taps. All its impurities, microorganisms, and bad smells are extracted. Rainwater, which is stored in special tanks, is also treated in the same way. The water is used at home for drinking, cooking, and washing.

Life in the Sea

A Thousand Forms of Life

The variety of plants and animals that we can see in the sea represents just a fraction of the great diversity of life that exists there. Even though the sea is not the richest biological environment, it does contain an immense assortment of plant and animal life.

Along with the best-known marine animals, there are thousands of other organisms that live under the sand at the bottom of the sea, in the seaweed, inside the holes of rocks, or within the bodies of other sea creatures.

The Food Chain

Marine animals, like all other living beings, must search for the food they need to survive in their environment. If we look closely at how one particular sea organism looks for food we will discover the beginnings of a sequence known as the food chain. Each and every organism, animal and plant, forms a link in the chain. In the sea there are thousands of such food chains made up by various species.

Most creatures of any food chain can feed off other chains as well. Such interactions—shown in the illustration with arrows—illustrate the formation of a food network.

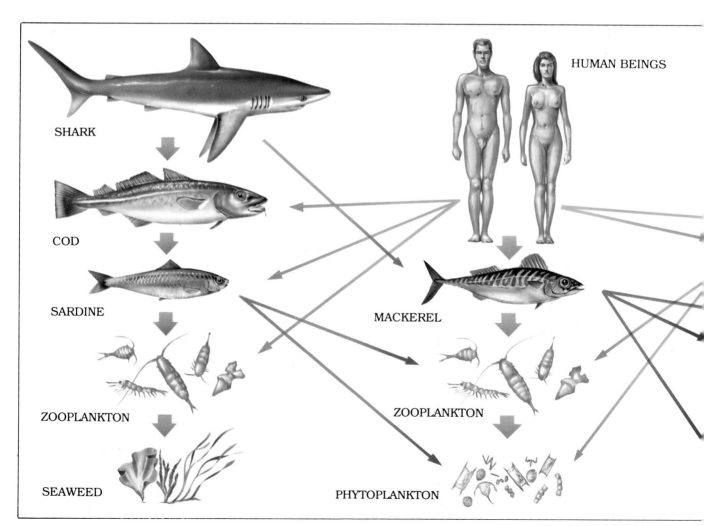

SHARK

COD

SARDINE

ZOOPLANKTON

SEAWEED

HUMAN BEINGS

MACKEREL

ZOOPLANKTON

PHYTOPLANKTON

The Links in the Chain

In every food chain we see that the animals have to search for food, since there is no animal that can produce it for itself. We also see that each chain always begins with a green plant.

In any chain the producer organism is the plant. The animals making up the rest of the links are called the consumer organisms.

The sea's main producer organism is phytoplankton. The primary consumers are zooplankton. The secondary and tertiary consumers are invertebrate marine creatures and fish of different sizes, and birds and mammals.

Sardines and anchovies feed on zooplankton. Tuna eat sardines, anchovies, and other species of fish, just like the shark, which also eats tuna. Anchovies, sardines, sharks, and many other fish form part of different chains. For this reason, when fish search for food, they establish a wide variety of relationships, creating a real food network.

The remains of creatures sink to the sea floor where they are transformed by bacteria into new matter that will in turn be used as food by phytoplankton. And then the process will start again.

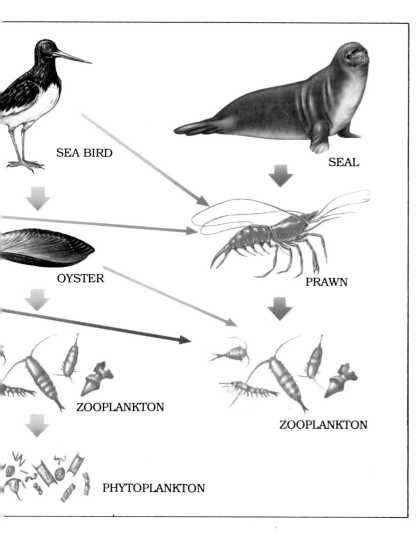

SEA BIRD

SEAL

OYSTER

PRAWN

ZOOPLANKTON

ZOOPLANKTON

PHYTOPLANKTON

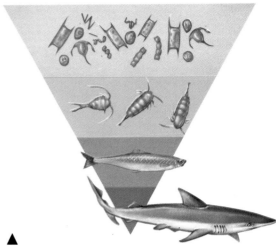

▲
When we talk about phytoplankton, we mean vegetable plankton, the sea's main food producer. Zooplankton, which are microscopic organisms that feed off sea plants, are the primary consumers. They serve as food for the secondary consumers (fish of varying sizes) who in turn are eaten by tertiary consumers such as cod and sharks. The number of large consumer species in each link in the chain progressively decreases, and so the food chain ends up looking something like an inverted pyramid.

In Search of Food

Life in the Sea

The life of an animal or a plant depends, to a certain extent, on the conditions of the place or ecosystem in which it lives. If we take the sea's ecosystem as an example we can see that the organisms that live in it have taken maximum advantage of their ecosystem.

One of the special characteristics of the sea's inhabitants is their increased capacity for reproduction. The millions and millions of sardines, mackerel, cod, and other fish that live in the sea are capable of producing hundreds of thousands of eggs every year.

But even the smallest plankton organisms can reproduce in the same numbers. In winter and in spring, when the deep waters of the sea rise to the surface carrying large quantities of nutrients, they reproduce at such a speed that in a short time the water takes on a greenish and sometimes reddish color as a result of the large number of microorganisms that have been produced.

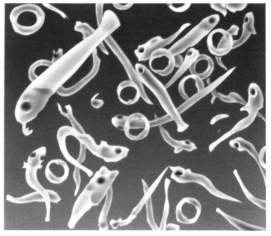

◀

Many animals that live in the sea are so small that it is only possible to see them through a microscope. All of these tiny animals together are called zooplankton. They eat phytoplankton, made up of millions of microscopic plants. The fish in turn feed on the zooplankton.

Species Distribution

At certain times of the year and in some areas the distribution of animals and vegetation is unequal. The fish that inhabit the water's surface, such as sardines and mackerel, are normally found in the most productive areas, that is to say, where there is abundant plankton for the fish to live on.

Bigger fish, such as tuna, travel long distances; their food source is not limited to one particular area.

The bodies of the fish that live near the surface of the sea, such as the mackerel, tend to be fusiform, rather like the shape of a cigar. ▼

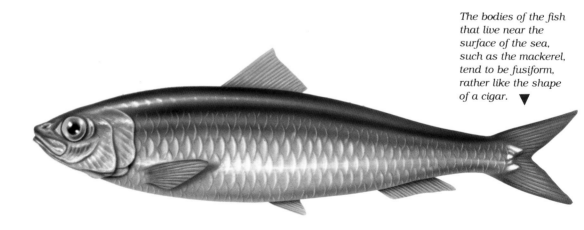

The air bladder and the fins are a fish's way of adapting to life in the sea. These are efficient adaptations to the problem of moving through water.
▼

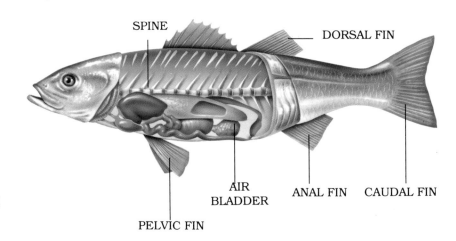

SPINE
DORSAL FIN
AIR BLADDER
ANAL FIN
CAUDAL FIN
PELVIC FIN

Survival in the Sea

Which species has the greatest chance of surviving when food is in short supply? It is the species with the widest range of food to choose from.

The sea is not a biologically diverse environment. Of the several million species inhabiting our planet, only 150,000 species live in the sea. For this reason, the sea's food chain is fragile and the alteration of just one of its links could be disastrous to many creatures.

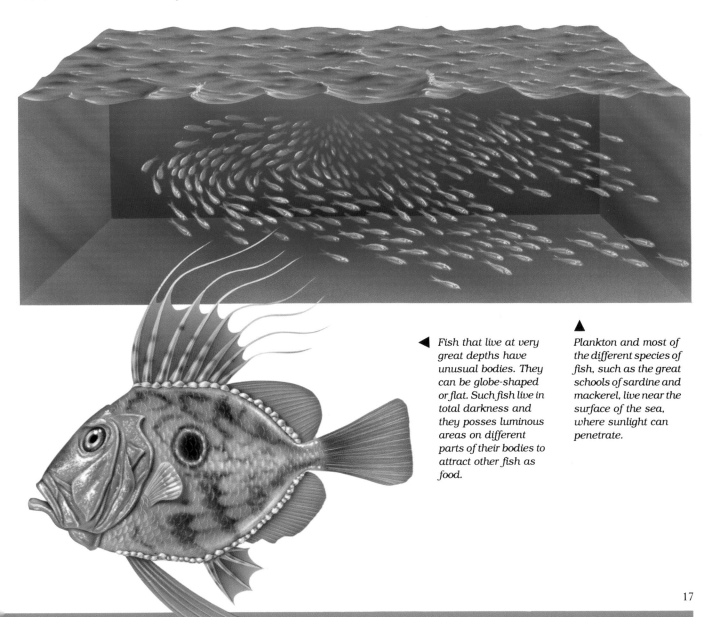

◀ *Fish that live at very great depths have unusual bodies. They can be globe-shaped or flat. Such fish live in total darkness and they posses luminous areas on different parts of their bodies to attract other fish as food.*

▲
Plankton and most of the different species of fish, such as the great schools of sardine and mackerel, live near the surface of the sea, where sunlight can penetrate.

The Sea's Resources

Oil

People have always exploited the sea's resources.

Deep under the sea floor lie deposits of oil, industrial civilization's main source of energy. From oil we obtain gasoline for cars and fuel for ships, airplanes, factories, and electrical generating stations. There are also secondary products made from oil, such as insecticides, detergents, and a great variety of plastics.

A fourth of the world's oil is being extracted from the bottom of the sea. New, more sophisticated techniques of oil extraction mean that we can drill deeper to find new deposits.

When oil started to become important in the developed world, construction began on bigger sea ports to help transport it. Shipbuilding adapted itself to this industry by constructing special oil tankers.

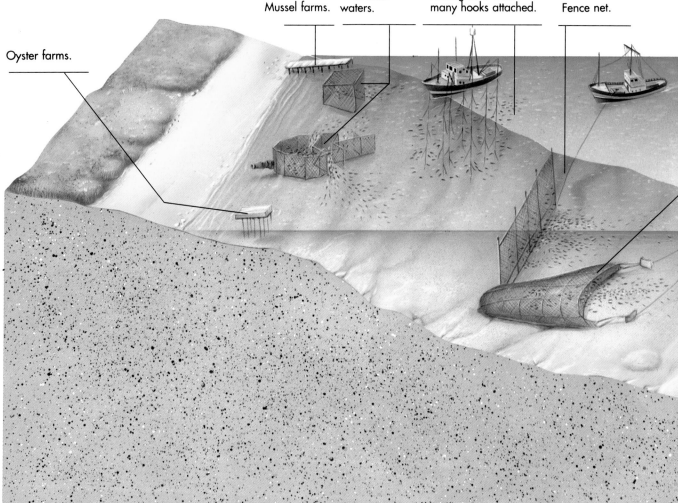

Oyster farms.

Mussel farms.

Nets attached to the bottom of coastal waters.

Fishing lines with many hooks attached.

Fence net.

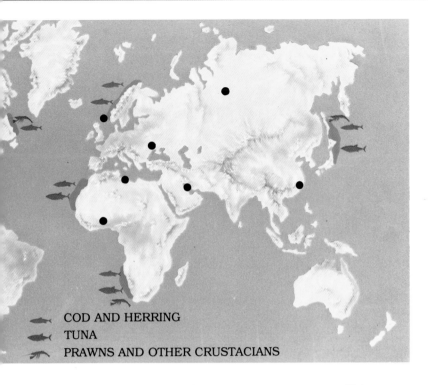

Fishing

Fishing is no longer a small-scale activity. It has been rapidly converted into an enormous industry that exploits the sea's resources for economic profit.

But marine creatures cannot reproduce themselves as fast as they are being harvested, and fish stocks are being depleted.

Fish are one of the most important resources of the sea. This illustration shows the different systems used for catching fish. ▼

◄ *This map shows the world's richest fishing grounds and major land and oceanic oil fields.*

➤ COD AND HERRING
➤ TUNA
➤ PRAWNS AND OTHER CRUSTACIANS

Sonar is used to detect the presence of schools of fish.

Drag net.

Ring net.

Hoist net.

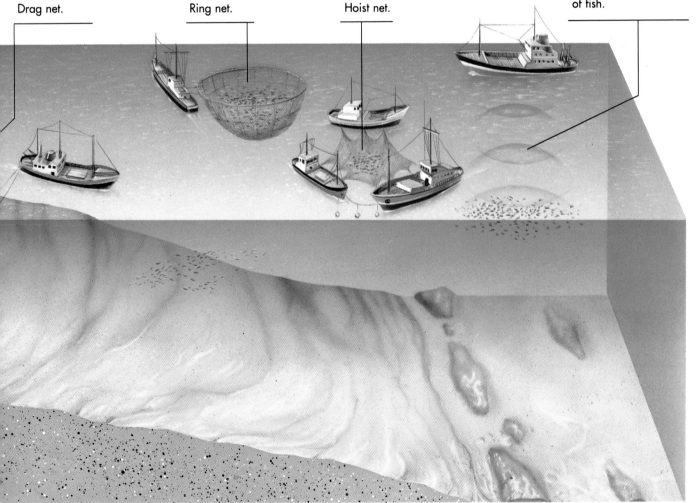

A Black Slick

Energy

In order to transform materials into the many products that people in the developed world have come to depend upon, industry requires energy. Almost every product and device in our homes and lives, from automobiles to furniture to fabrics, is shaped or constructed through the expenditure of energy, and most often the source of that energy is oil.

Transporting Oil

Oil has to be transported from pumping sites to industrial areas, however far apart they may be. A third of the earth's oil travels the sea lanes of the world by ship. When an accident occurs, oil spills into the sea, causing an oil slick, which can spread out over a wide area.

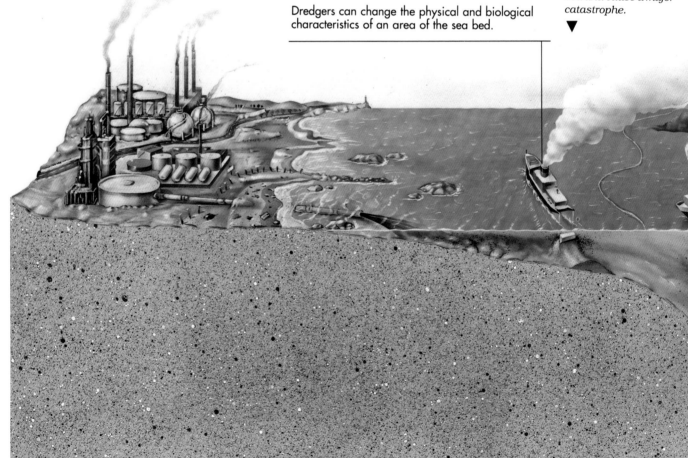

Dredgers can change the physical and biological characteristics of an area of the sea bed.

One of the sea's greatest pollutants is oil. If an oil tanker has an accident, its load can spill out into the sea and cause a major catastrophe.

▼

Refineries transform and purify crude oil in order to obtain different products such as gasoline, ethylene, and propylene. The products obtained from oil refineries are used in the making of plastics, synthetic fibers, medicine, dyes, and detergents.

An oil tanker accident. Special boats extinguish oil flames and floating barriers are placed around the slick to stop it from spreading and reaching the coast. Chemicals and even bacteria are used to disperse or consume the oil.

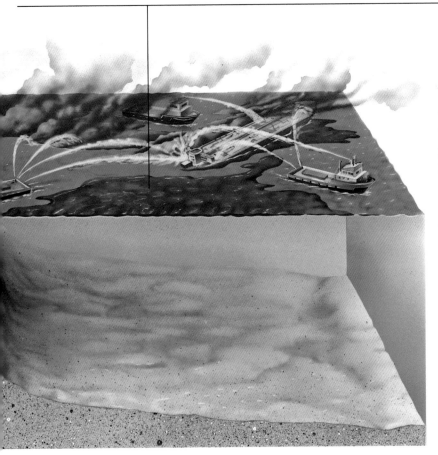

The Ecological Consequences

The oil slick prevents light from penetrating the sea, which in turn prevents plankton from developing and damages the food chain. Furthermore, oil is toxic and kills sea life.

The tar from the oil can slowly sink to the bottom of the sea, preventing the marine current from transporting mineral substances from the depths to the sea surface. Finally, we must not forget about the damage to beaches and costal areas, as well as the threat to fish and birds.

Sea Pollutants

Improving Crops

With the aim of getting the maximum yield from crops and combating the diseases that can ruin them, farmers apply to their fields chemical products known as fertilizers and pesticides.

About one hundred years ago, one of the best known pesticides, DDT, began to be used. It was absorbed through the skin of insects, causing their almost instant death.

But DDT also affected other animals. It caused birds to lay eggs whose shells were so thin that they broke before chicks hatched. DDT had the same effect on the shells of mollusks in the sea.

By Way of Rivers

Rainwater washes the fertilizers and insecticides used by farmers down to rivers. The rivers carry them downstream to the sea.

Fertilizers and pesticides do not degrade easily. They remain in the water, where they can be swallowed by marine life.

These substances then begin to circulate through the food chain and their effects are apparent in its different links, from plankton to fish. Through contaminated fish, it finally reaches human beings.

Intensive use of crop fertilizer in order to combat famine—in a world with a population bordering on six billion people—and the use of insecticides to control pests can create serious pollution problems.

There are many different sources of marine pollution. In the illustration you can see some of the main causes of contamination.

▼

SOME OF THE PRINCIPLE FORMS OF OCEAN POLLUTION

Nuclear power stations use water to cool their reactors. Hot water can alter the life cycle of certain marine organisms when it reaches the sea.

Run-off from fields carries fertilizers and pesticides into the river.

Industrial complexes empty chemical products into the rivers.

◀

The use of insecticides in agriculture can create pollution in the sea. Rain carries the contaminated water to rivers, and rivers carry the chemicals to the sea. Crop spraying, like that performed by the plane in the illustration, often requires larger amounts and more lethal types of pesticides as insects develop resistance to them.

Certain factories release toxic wastes directly into the sea.

Solid wastes, such as plastic and glass, pollute beaches.

The burning and dumping of wastes on the high seas, the cleaning of oil tankers, and accidental spillage are other forms of ocean pollution. Microorganisms that absorb or digest these pollutants are often overwhelmed and cannot purify the water and restore its natural composition.

Sewage

Polluted Water

Sea water is polluted when it contains substances that cause the loss of its natural characteristics. For example:
—When the oxygen that marine creatures need to breath is lacking.
—When ocean water contains insecticides or radioactive fallout.
—When oil or tar prevent plankton from developing the nutrients that other organisms on the food chain need.
—When the nutrient renewal process of upwelling currents is cut off.

In summary, water is polluted when the relationships between plankton and light, plankton and other marine organism, and the sea bed and the surface are damaged.

The Causes of Pollution

Many pollutants reach the sea as a consequence of human activity.

Rivers carry the fertilizers and insecticides used in agriculture into the sea. They also transport toxic waste from the factories placed on their banks. Villages and towns throw their sewage into the rivers and seas.

Purifying the Water

Both industrial waste and sewage are pollutants. This is why it is necessary to cleanse water before it renters the water cycle through rivers, seas, and clouds.

The process of cleansing depends on the level and the type of pollutant. Some of these processes are very complex and expensive.

Water must go through the following processes to be purified:
—Solid waste and larger particles must be

One way to reduce marine pollution is to cleanse the sewage from the waste water of large towns. By treating sewage in purification plants, it is possible to restore to waste water its natural characteristics before it flows into the sea.

▼

HOW A WATER PURIFICATION PLANT WORKS

Sewage enters the purifying plant.

A series of filters removes materials of a large size, such as plastic and rags.

Heavy particles settle out as sediment at the bottom of special tanks.

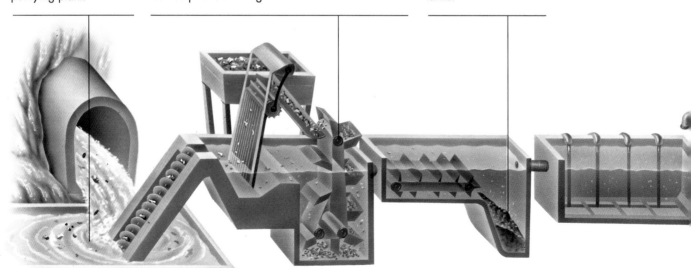

filtered out and separated.
—Smaller particles are allowed to settle at the bottom of tanks or cisterns as slime or mud.
—Other particles suspended in the water are removed through further filtration and coagulation, that is, by bonding the pollutants to heavier particles that settle out as sediment.
—The purified water is drained through submerged pipes that carry it a certain distance from the shore in order to disperse it into the sea water.

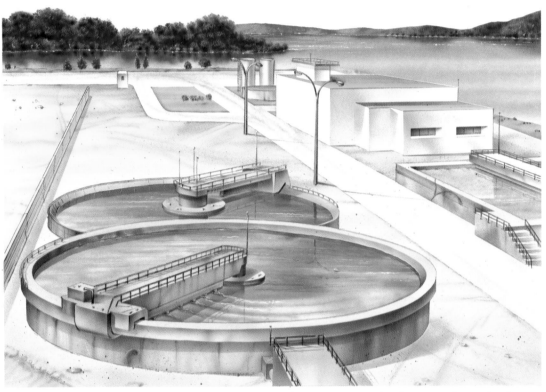

◀

Water that has been used in cities and factories is piped through sewer systems until it finally reaches the river or the sea. Because of increasing levels of pollutants, water must be treated in purification plants, such as the one in the illustration, to get rid of toxic substances.

In well-aerated tanks or cisterns, the proper conditions for the development of microorganisms are created. These microorganisms decompose the organic matter in water.

The water is treated with various chemicals whose function is to bond with pollutants and form larger clots of material that are easier to separate from the water.

The water treated in the purification plant is returned to the rivers and the sea in a clean condition.

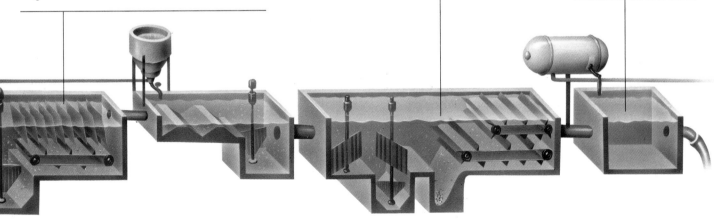

Between the Land and the Sea

How a Delta is Formed

A delta is the result of the slow accumulation of materials that have been brought downriver by the current. These materials generally consist of fine particles such as sand and sludge. Bigger particles are left upstream.

The force of the seawater disperses some of these materials, which then form littorals and lagoons. Meanwhile, the river continues to bring more materials.

In the delta there is a constant battle between seawater and fresh water to gain a hold on the area. The biggest deltas are always found where the sea is calm.

Who Lives in a Delta?

The lagoons, salt marshes, flooded areas, and sand dunes form an ecosystem that is rich in birds, insects, and plants. Crustaceans, fish, and sea plankton are also found in the delta, which is an ideal place for living and reproducing.

Migrating birds from other parts of the world use the delta as a resting place. When they have regained their strength they continue on to warmer climates where they will lay their eggs.

The delta consists of successive layers of sediments, brought down the river and dispersed on the bottom of the sea.

▼

EGRET

GAMBUSIA

The land area of the delta gradually pushes out over the sea.

The delta supports a unique group of creatures, small fish that feed on insect larvae and specially adapted birds that feed on the small fish.

Fertile materials transported down the river to an easily irrigated region convert the delta into a fertile area for agriculture.

Rice is cultivated under a shallow layer of water.

The Delta's Value

Deltas posses unique characteristics of dampness and rich soils, and are thoroughly exploited by a variety of creatures, including human beings.

Deltas such as the one at the mouth of the river Nile have been the object of cleaning projects. Small organisms and mosquitoes (transmitters of illnesses like malaria) have been eradicated. Pumping stations have been installed to enable stagnant waters to circulate constantly.

The constant flow of fertile materials brought down the river makes the delta a region rich in good farmland. A great variety of vegetables and cereals, such as rice, are grown in the areas between the river and the sea.

The delta has suffered for this, since human intervention has transformed it from a home to wildlife into a mainly agricultural area.

Most plants living in the delta have air conduits and chambers in their stems and their leaves that allow them to take in the necessary oxygen when their roots are submerged in the water. However, if the water level goes down, they can survive long periods of dryness.

The water's movements disperse the fine materials brought down the river and the accumulating sediments form islands, channels, and lakes.

Birds live in the delta, where abundant insects and plants with seeds provide food.

The delta tends to form a network of crisscrossing forks and channels that slow down the river's main currents.

MARSH PLANT

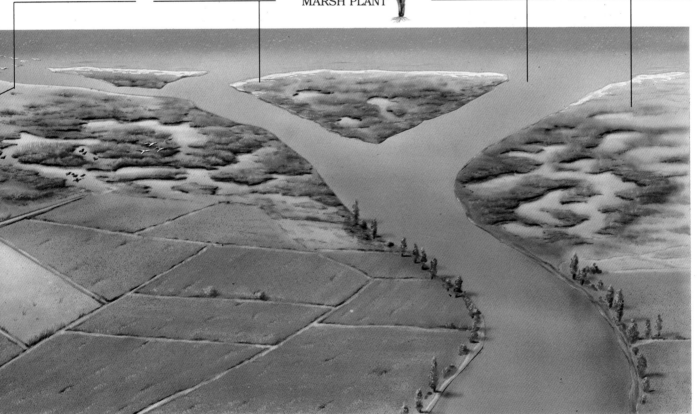

Activities

Oil and Water Don't Mix

The oil dumped by tankers on the high seas or the millions of gallons spilled after an accident will remain afloat. Oil does not mix with water because it is not as dense; it is lighter and will float on water. You can produce a similar effect with this simple experiment.

a measuring cup

MATERIALS

1. Pour some oil into a measuring cup. Cooking oil will do.

▼

a glass of cold water

a bottle of oil

2. Then add a similar amount of water.

▼

3. The oil is less dense than the water, so it floats on top.

▼

Water Purification

You can construct a water purification plant in your own house. It will help you to understand how water can regain its natural properties. To carry out this experiment, you first have to dirty the water you are going to purify. Mix it together with some milk, oil, sand, and so on.

MATERIALS

sand

coal

cotton wool

bleach

plastic bottle

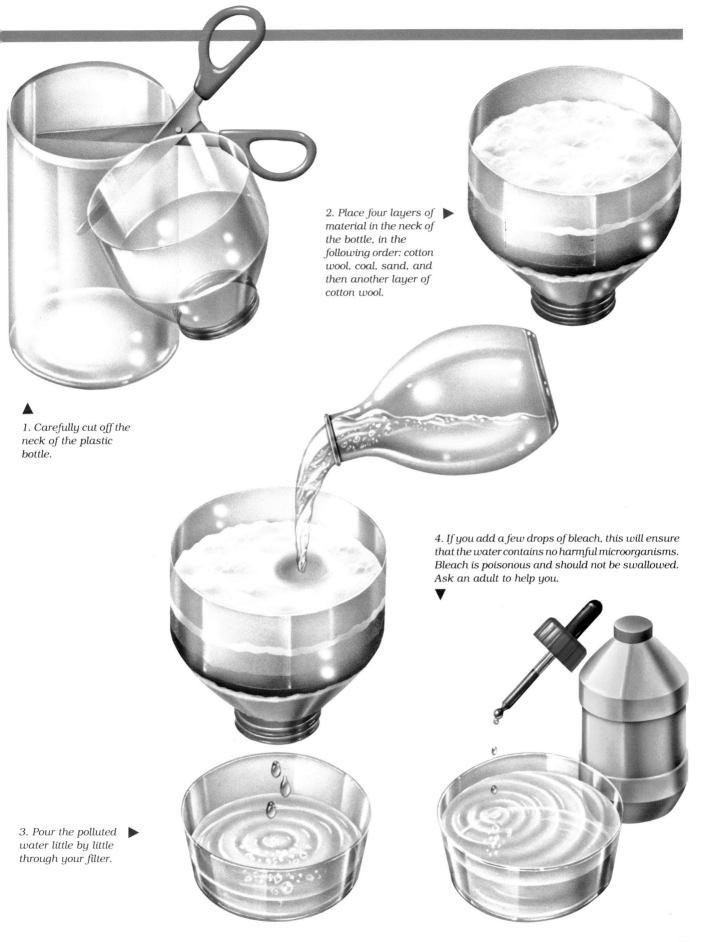

1. Carefully cut off the neck of the plastic bottle.

2. Place four layers of material in the neck of the bottle, in the following order: cotton wool, coal, sand, and then another layer of cotton wool.

3. Pour the polluted water little by little through your filter.

4. If you add a few drops of bleach, this will ensure that the water contains no harmful microorganisms. Bleach is poisonous and should not be swallowed. Ask an adult to help you.

Words to Remember

Community A group of animal and plant organisms that occupy a specific area.

Food chain The transfer of food, or energy, from one group of organisms to another. Each group makes up a link in the chain. Each link receives energy from the previous link and at the same time provides energy to the following link.

Minerals Minerals come from decomposing organic matter. Plants absorb them from the ground. They are essential for the creation of organic matter.

Organic matter Matter made from living organisms.

Plankton A group of organisms that live floating in the sea. They are made up of small animals (zooplankton) and plants (phytoplankton).They are the food for many larger marine animals.

Photosynthsis The process by which plants make food. This happens when they use the energy of sunlight to assimilate and transform water and carbon dioxide into food and new plant tissue.

Radioactive waste Substances that emit high energy particles and rays as they disintegrate. Some types of radioactive waste are extremely dangerous.

Sewage Water that contains different kinds of waste from agriculture, industry, and cities. It is often discharged into rivers or the sea.

Upwelling The vertical movement of seawater that allows the water at the bottom of the ocean to mix with surface water. Minerals can thus get to plankton at the surface.

Water pollution The presence of alien substances that affect the properties and quality of water and the lives of the organisms living in it.

Index

DATE DUE

AP 25 00			